MW01171827

NARCISSISM OF RELIGION

The Cycle of Control and Abuse

Dearyl W. Moore Jr

TABLE OF CONTENT
Narcissism of Religion

The Cycle of Control and Abuse

INTRODUCTION

Narcissism of Religion
The Cycle of Control and Abuse

I've spent much of my adult life studying religion. Many years ago I came into the life changing revelation that there is a massive difference between religion and the Kingdom of God. This may already be something you're very familiar with or you might be wondering what in the world I'm talking about right now. I'm going to assume this is a new revelation to you and break it down into more detail.

I spent most of my life growing up in the Pentecostal movement and you might imagine I thought I knew everything. But I noticed that the church seemed to have no true power and authority. I had read in the Bible where Jesus said we would do even greater works than even He had done Himself. But in reality we were seeing little to no change in church. Out of frustration I really started to press in to God about what was going on in our modern day churches. What God began to reveal to me literally shocked me and changed my life.

Religion was never God's intent for His Children. The Bible teaches something absolutely different. In Matthew 6:33 KJV we are told "But **seek ye first the kingdom of God**, and his righteousness; and all these things shall be added unto you". It's interesting that we were not told to seek religion. Why does it not say seek religion? What is religion? Where did religion come from?

I have met so many people in my life that have shared their stories of how they were deeply hurt by a religious church or a religious leader or even just a religious person. Most recently I was speaking with a lady nearly eighty years old and she told me how she had planned to crash her car into the front of the church and commit suicide just to show them how much they had hurt her.

In another situation I was called to pray with an elderly man that was given just a short time to live. During our conversation he told me of how he was attending a church and his brother died but he had no financial means to travel out of town for his funeral. He said he actually shared his need with his pastor and the pastor requested that he work on his tractor and when he finished the pastor never said another word about helping him financially. The elderly man said that he was broken and just cried over the death of his brother and the lack of compassion shown by his pastor. The elderly man looked at me and said the church wasn't even real anymore and there were no real pastors anymore. I could go on and on with stories just like these. Maybe you've even heard one like these or maybe you have your own story.

My first book I ever wrote is called "Coup d'état" which explores and explains religion and the history of religion in much more detail than I intend to do in this book. But if you're interested in a more detailed study of religion please check out my other book. Many of the points that I'll be making about religion here will be mostly from my first book.

So if you're ready here we go. I hope by time you finish reading this book you will be much more informed on the nature and origin of religion.

CHAPTER 1

What is Religion?

If you take a moment and do a basic google search on the word religion this is what you might get, "Religion is a set of organized beliefs, practices, and systems that most often relate to the belief and worship of a controlling force, such as a personal god or another supernatural being". Sounds kinda mystical and harmless so far, right? What was the first religion? Let's do another google search.

Stibich, Mark Phd "What Is Religion?" Very Well Mind Updated on November 14, 2022 November 14, 2022 https://www.verywellmind.com/religion-improves-health-2224007

Based upon another google search. Hinduism is the world's oldest religion, according to many scholars, with roots and customs dating back more than 4,000 years. Today, with about 900 million followers, Hinduism is the third-largest religion behind Christianity and Islam. Roughly 95 percent of the world's Hindus live in India.

History.com Editors, "Hinduism" HISTORY October 6, 2017, Update May 19, 2022, 2022

November 14, 2022 https://www.history.com/topics/religion/hinduism

So maybe you thought Christianity was the first known religion. Nope, Christianity is only considered to be one of many religions taught throughout the world today. Actually there are currently considered to be somewhere around 4,000 different world religions. Of these major religions, Christianity is the largest, with more than two billion followers.

Christianity is based on the life and teachings of Jesus Christ and is approximately 2,000 years old. But a staggering statistic is that there are currently estimated to be approximately 45,000 documented different denominations of Christianity in the world today. I find this alarming as a Christian when we look at Matthew 12:25 KJV "And Jesus knew their thoughts, and said unto them, Every kingdom divided against itself is brought to desolation; and every city or house divided against itself shall not stand." This was Jesus talking here, and He said a house divided against itself shall not stand. So why would we not take this seriously?

Every Sunday, Wednesday and maybe other days people all over America in small towns to large cities gather in buildings in the pretense of a religious experience. Most of these American gatherings are considered to be based on Christianity in nature. People gather, they sing spiritual songs, someone usually stands behind a pulpit preaching a message and the cycle repeats week after week. But might I add this is considered to also be the most segregated times in America.

Most Americans, if asked, will say they are religious in some way or the other. So religion as stated earlier is "Religion is a set of organized beliefs, practices, and systems that most often relate to the belief and worship of a controlling force, such as a personal god or another supernatural being". So religion as defined is not a specific belief or devotion but rather just the idea that can be expressed in many different ways. Buddhists are religious, Hindus are religious, Satanists are religious in that they all believe in and worship what they consider to be a superhuman controlling power.

Tomorrow it seems that any of us could start a new religion. For example, there is this new thing going on in the internet world known as the metaverse. So to get a jump on things we could start a new and exciting religious movement called the Meta-God. The god that rules the virtual experiences. I can assure you that in no time at all we could generate a following. But does the worship of something make it real? Does worshiping something give it real power here in the realm of earth. Does worshiping something or becoming religious about something make it real.

I think the reality of religion is that it's just a belief or worship of something real or unreal. So being religious within itself doesn't make someone an actual Christian. Being a religious Christian just means that you are religious in your pursuit of the teachings of Christ or the study of the beliefs of the Bible.

The word religion does not mean Christian or Christianity nor does the word Christian mean religion. Religion is simply the passionate belief or pursuit of something. In that understanding someone can be religious about football, baseball, money or many other things in the world. Maybe you can take just a moment and ask yourself what things in life are you religious about?

CHAPTER 2

The Neutrality of Religion

It's at this point you might be wondering if religion is a good thing or a bad thing. So let us take a look at both sides of religion before we rush to a conclusion. First of all let us take a look at some of the good points about religion.

Samaritan's Purse

When we look at the Christian religious organization Samaritan's Purse under the leadership of Franklin Graham, who is the son of the former Evangelist Billy Graham there is no way to deny the good of this organization. Information from their website samaritanspurse.org indicates that they have approximately 150,000 volunteers and ministry partners in more than 100 countries.

They specialize in meeting critical needs for victims of war, disaster, and famine in the world's most troubled regions, often working through local churches and ministry partners. Since 1998 they have helped almost 40,000 families that were impacted by U.S. natural disasters —hurricanes, tornadoes, wildfires, floods, and ice storms—by quickly providing emergency supplies and cleaning, repairing and rebuilding homes.

In 2017 they responded to the areas in Texas and Florida due to hurricane damage and helped more that 3,600 families recover from the damages of the storms. Most recently they began helping about 1,000 Texas families get back into their homes through rebuilding homes, repairs or by providing materials. They also have a medical assistance program that has brought more than 1,200 children with heart defects to North America to receive life-saving surgeries in partnership with approximately 66 hospitals.

Since 1993, Samaritan's Purse through their Operation Christmas Child has delivered more than 157 million shoebox gifts to children in more than 160 countries and territories. There are many other amazing things this organization has done and continues to do all over the world on a daily basis.

Samaritan's Purse "Samaritan's Purse Overview Fact Sheet" Samaritan's Purse International Relief November 14, 2022 https://www.samaritanspurse.org/our-ministry/

samaritans-purse-overview-fact-sheet/

Salvation Army

Since 1878 the Salvation Army founded by William and Catherine Booth has been a powerful difference maker in the world. From the moment they penned the original name in 1878 they were able to lead more than 250,00 people to Christ from just 1881 to 1885. If you've even been shopping around Christmas time there is no doubt you've seen the iconic Salvation Army red kettle. This is a program that was started in 1891 by Captain Joseph McFee.

Captain McFee was an officer in the Salvation Army and he was looking for a way to simply cover the cost of the community Christmas meal. This tradition originally started when he placed a pot at the Oakland Ferry Landing, at the foot of Market Street where it could be seen by all those going to the ferry boats. By 1895 the "kettle" was used by 30 locations along the west coast and by 1897 the campaign was on the rise in the east. This tradition continues to this very day. The donations they raise yearly help care for the homeless and needy all over the world as well as helping more than 30 million people through a variety of other services.

The iconic Salvation Army red kettle campaign began in 1891 by Captain Joseph McFee, a Salvation Army officer who was looking for a way to cover the cost of the community Christmas meal. Recalling his days as a sailor in Liverpool, England, he recreated the "Simpson's Pot", an iron pot where charitable donations were placed by passersby. Captain McFee placed a similar pot at the Oakland Ferry Landing, at the foot of Market Street where it could be seen by all those going to and from the ferry boats.

By 1895 the 'kettle' was used by 30 locations along the west coast and by 1897 the campaign was making its mark in the east. That year, the kettle effort in Boston and other locations nationwide resulted in 150,000 Christmas dinners for the needy. The tradition continues still today. Sharing your donation at Christmastime helps The Salvation Army care for homeless and needy families, but also helps serve 30 million people through a myriad of other services all year long.

Salvation Army "About US" The Salvation Army November 14, 2022 https://www.salvationarmyusa.org/usn/about/

There is no question that many Christian religious organizations have and continue to do amazing work all over the world every single day. There are many other tremendous organizations just like the ones I just highlighted working to make a positive difference as well. So as we can see there is a good side of religion. So with that said let us look to see if there's a bad side of religion again I'm going to focus within the parameters of Christianity.

Jonestown

There was a man by the name of Jim Jones who in 1954 founded The People's Temple Full Gospel Church in Indianapolis, Indiana. This was founded as a Christian organization with communist and socialist ideology and an emphasis on racial equality. In 1960 Jones moved the organization to California and established several locations throughout the state with its headquarters being in San Francisco. During this time the organization established many relationships with left-wing political figures and estimated its members to be approximately 20,000. Most resources estimate the actual number to be more accurately estimated between

3,000 to 5,000.

In 1974, Jones leased a piece of property in Guyana and established a community which was named the Peoples Temple Agricultural Project or better known as "Jonestown". To Jones he viewed this as a sanctuary and a social paradise far away from the pressures of the normal world and the media hounds. This was a small group of people in the beginning with an estimated group of about fifty in early 1977. In 1978 due to political pressure Jones influenced a large group of his U.S. based followers to move to Jonestown in Guyana with him. This request had increased the population to approximately 900 people by late 1978. He accomplished this increase by promising a tropical paradise free from the supposed wickedness of the outside world to everyone who journeyed with him.

It was on November 17, 1978 that a US Representative by the name of Leo Ryan visited Jonestown to investigate claims of abuse filed. It was during his visit that some of the occupants of Jonestown requested that they be able to leave with him. The next day, November 18th some of them went with Ryan to the local airstrip. During this time the group was encountered by security guards from Jonestown who then opened fire on the group, killing Leo Ryan, three of the journalists as well as one of the people trying to escape. Nine other people were also injured during this time.

Later that evening Jim Jones ordered all the members of Jonestown to drink a deadly grape flavored concoction that was laced with cyanide. That evening 918 people died as a result of religion gone wrong, including 271 children. Some of the members that tried to resist the orders were injected against their with a fatal cyanide dose. This event stood as the great deliberate act of American death up until the September 11 attacks on the twin towers in 2001. Wikipedia, "The Peoples Temple" Wikipedia the free encyclopedia November 14, 2022 https://en.wikipedia.org/wiki/Peoples_Temple

Waco

In 1959 a child was born by the name of Vernon Wayne Howell in Houston Texas to a 15 year old mother. He never knew his father and was raised by his grandparents. He would later become known by the name of David Koresh. David said that his childhood was lonely and that other kids picked on him often. In his own words he wasn't a good student for the most part and ended up dropping out of high school. The only thing he thought he was interested in was the bible and music.

Around the age of 20, David got involved with his mother's church, the Seventh Day Adventist. But this didn't go much better than school in that he was kicked out for being a bad influence upon other kids. He finally decided to pursue his musical talents and moved off to Hollywood to pursue his dreams. The pursuit of being a rockstar seemed to fall flat as well as nothing ever developed for him in music either. It was finally around 1981 that David moved to Waco Texas to join a religious group known as the Branch Davidians. This was a religious organization that was established in the area of Waco as early as 1935 and at its peak boasted more than 1,400 members.

It didn't take long for trouble to follow David as it was believed he was having an affair with Lois Roden who was considered to be a prophetess in her late sixties at this time. It was documented that they had even traveled to Israel together. This entire ordeal had created tremendous conflict between David and Roden's son George causing David to move away with some of his devout followers. This disagreement continued and finally culminated in 1987 when he returned to Mount Carmel with seven of his followers all dressed in camouflage and armed with rifles and shotguns. The conflict erupted into a gunfight eventually leaving the son "George" of David's former lover wounded in his chest and hands.

It was around 1990 that David had finally become the leader of the Branch Davidians and he legally changed his name in a court document citing that it was for publicity and business purposes. David being his new name was to line up with the fact that he believed he was now the true leader of the biblical house of David.

All of this finally came to an end in what has been called the Waco siege or the Waco massacre. A siege was conducted upon the compound that belonged to the religious organization called the Branch Davidians. It was carried out by the U.S. federal government, U.S. military and Texas state law enforcement; the entire event took place from February 28 to April 19, 1993.

The event started when the ATF attempted to serve a search warrant as well as an arrest warrant at the ranch. During this attempt a violent gunfight erupted that initially resulted in the deaths of four law enforcement officers and six members of the Branch Davidians. But this was only the beginning of what would develop into a horrible situation.

The failure to to execute the search warrant and arrest warrant started what would become a siege and standoff that would last 51 days. Eventually, the FBI launched an assault with the use of tear gas in hopes of forcing members of the Branch Davidians out of the ranch. But this resulted in the compound becoming engulfed in flames. The fire resulted in the deaths of 75 Branch Davidians, including 25 children, two pregnant women and the leader David Koresh. Wikipedia, "Waco siege" Wikipedia the free encyclopedia November 14, 2022 https:// en.wikipedia.org/wiki/Waco_siege

Again this just stands as another horrible example of religion when it all goes the wrong way. So we have now seen religion being used for good and the result of religion when it goes bad. So we can now say that religion itself is not good or bad but the word religion can be applied to the nature of the ones operating under the definition of religion. So being religious doesn't make one good or bad, it all depends on how religion is applied. So religion is neutral in nature one might say.

CHAPTER 3

The Spirit of Religion

As I've stated earlier I have studied religion for most of my adult life. I wouldn't consider myself an expert in religion but I would say that I'm very well informed on the idea of religion. During my studies I received revelation to something I discovered called the spirit of religion. With this being said I'm not even sure if you can actually consider religion neutral when you really consider the author of religion and the nature of religion.

The spirit of religion is actually rooted in Satan himself, remember he got kicked out of heaven for desiring to be worshiped taking a third of the angels with him. Satan from the very beginning has desired to be worshiped, thus creating a form of godliness that has no power. So religion has always been on the earth. There were countless false religions before Jesus was born. But the presence of Jesus exposed them all.

In studying religion, the history of religion and the origin of religion I came across the most disturbing discovery of my life. The greatest enemy of God's Church on earth is actually the work of a <u>Religious Spirit.</u> You may be asking, what in the world is a religious spirit? The most important thing you have to understand is that a **religious spirit is a demonic spirit**. It is the most dangerous of all demonic spirits. Jesus defined three demonic spirits in Revelation chapter 2 and 3. He said that they would totally control and dominate the church during the last days. Let's look at the spirits and where they're found in the book of Revelation. First in Revelation 2:14 "But I have a few things against thee, because thou hast there them that hold the doctrine of **Balaam**, who taught Balac to cast a stumbling block before the children of Israel, to eat things sacrificed unto idols, and to commit fornication."

Second, Revelation 2:20-21 "Notwithstanding I have a few things against thee, because thou sufferest that woman **Jezebel**, which calleth herself a prophetess, to teach and to seduce my servants to commit fornication, and to eat things sacrificed unto idols. And I gave her space to repent of her fornication; and she repented not.

Lastly in Revelation 2:15-16 "So hast thou

also them that hold the doctrine of the **Nicolaitanes**, which thing I hate. Repent; or else I will come unto thee quickly, and will fight against them with the sword of my mouth." And there you have the 3 strand cord that can't be easily broken known as the Religious Spirit, or the Trinity of the kingdom of darkness.

Satan is the enemy to the Kingdom of God and his desire is to totally destroy the kingdom of God. We should not be surprised that we encounter demonic spirits operating inside the church today. Satan has long been aware of the fact that the church was originally designed to destroy the works of his kingdom. But something has happened within the church, where is the power and authority? The Bible has already foretold of a day where there would be complete departure that would be so great that those who hear the spirit of truth, will hear Him saying come out of her my people, and commanding His people to withdraw themselves from such false teachers. (Rev 18:4) & (1 Tim 6:5)

The religious spirit is the oldest and most experienced of the demonic spirits. It has desired to be worshiped from its very foundation in heaven. The religious spirit has defeated Kings,

Popes, Preachers, governments and churches. We see it show up in the Old Testament. Abel had offered his sacrifice with reverence and obedient faith, obeying God. But the old religious spirit overcame Cain and his focus became about the works rather than obedience. Cain made his offering out of performance instead of faith and obedience.

No wonder so many modern churches are so performance driven. This early account of Cain and Abel shows us the very nature of the religious spirit, it is to deceive you into believing that there is another way other than God's way. In the Garden of Eden, Eve was questioned regarding the word of God. Satan was the root of the question and deception. The religious spirit was and still is the greatest tool Satan uses to bring forth deception and disobedience. It's our greatest enemy to the truth of God's Kingdom.

The Religious Spirit is made up of these three spirits. The first is the spirit of **Balaam**. The nature of this spirit is to create division and prevent unity in the body of Christ. This spirit will label people to create differences. The very nature of this spirit is to appeal to anyone that has an itching ear to hear only what they want to hear. This spirit will divide a group of people on the basis of age, gender, race, doctrine, social economical and as many ways as possible. One of the first things to look for Satan to attack with is division.

The second spirit that makes up a religious spirit is the spirit of **Nicolaitans**. This spirit has the absolute nature to conquer God's people. The very essence of this spirit is total control of God's house and God's people. This is contrary to the nature of God, greatness is learned from being a servant not a dictator. Once people are divided, always watch out for Satan's attempt to conquer.

The third spirit that makes up a religious spirit is the spirit of **Jezebel**. The nature of this spirit is to seek out the leaders and destroy them. The spirit can use the tactic of seduction in many ways for the purpose of death. Many times spiritual death, not physical but physical, is always an option. The Jezebel spirit will entice religious people in the church to fall in love with something other than Jesus Himself thus committing spiritual adultery. Together these spirits make a three strand cord because Satan knows it's not easily broken.

Even Satan knows the Word of God is true.

Using the very principle taught in Ecclesiastes: "Thought one may be overpowered, two can defend themselves. A cord of three strands is not quickly broken." (Ecclesiastes 4:12 NIV) These three spirits operate as one to not only imitate the trinity but to divide, conquer, and kill the body of Christ knowing it won't be easily broken.

The religious spirit receives its direction from the oldest of all spirits, the **spirit of Pride**. This is the very spirit that caused Lucifer to get kicked out of heaven as well as man being kicked out of Eden. Pride will cause you to align yourself against the purpose of God. Pride will isolate you, causing you to believe that you're the only one that can be right. Pride will make you believe that your way of having church is the only way that pleases God.

The spirit of pride will cause you to be too proud to admit that you're wrong. Pride will cause us to focus on differences and miss out on unity. Pride will cause you to trust the vote of man more than than the will of God. Pride says I will trust money more than the creator of all things. Pride will always create an atmosphere that is deadly to heavenly things. Pride must die for heaven to live. You will always find prideful people and prideful churches to be the hardest to reach.

So you may be wondering, how did I see this religious spirit? The Bible says that Satan is a deceiver and an imitator. Satan has a pattern of imitating everything that God has created. To Christians the cross is a sign of victory, but Satan imitates it as a sign of defeat. To Christians the rainbow is a covenant sign that God will never destroy the earth again, but Satan uses it as a sign of victory for the LGBT.

So now religion doesn't look so innocent or neutral. No doubt there are good people who operate inside of the parameters of religion but I have found no good intent when looking at religion or more specifically the spirit of religion. The origin and nature of religion is very demonic. I would go as far to say that Christianity should not be considered a religion or religious, once it becomes religious it is corrupt or one might even say evil. The author of religion is none other than Satan himself.

CHAPTER 4

Narcissism of Religion

The basic definition of narcissism is someone who has an excessive interest in or admiration of themselves. With this in mind let us look at the scripture Isaiah 14:13-16 KJV "10 All they shall speak and say unto thee, Art thou also become weak as we? art thou become like unto us? 11 Thy pomp is brought down to the grave, *and* the noise of thy viols: the worm is spread under thee, and the worms cover thee. 12 How art thou fallen from heaven, O Lucifer, son of the morning! *how* art thou cut down to the ground, which didst weaken the nations! 13 For thou hast said in thine heart, I will ascend into heaven, <u>I will exalt my throne above the stars of God</u>: I will sit also upon the mount of the congregation, in the sides of the north: 14 I will ascend above the heights of the clouds; I will be like the most High. 15 Yet thou shalt be brought down to hell, to the sides of the pit. 16 They that see thee shall narrowly look upon thee, *and* consider thee, *saying, Is* this the man that made the earth to tremble, that did shake kingdoms".

Here we clearly see Satan himself desiring to exalt himself above the throne of God. He saw himself above God, greater than God.

Once again we look at the scriptures Matthew 4:8-10   "8 Again, the devil taketh him up into an exceeding high mountain, and sheweth him all the kingdoms of the world, and the glory of them; 9 And saith unto him, All these things will I give thee, if thou wilt fall down and worship me. 10 Then saith Jesus unto him, Get thee hence, Satan: for it is written, Thou shalt worship the Lord thy God, and him only shalt thou serve."

There is no question that Lucifer also known as Satan has always had the desire to be worshiped and exalted above all. So when he fell it would only be expected that he would desire to be worshiped. He wasn't able to exalt himself above God and have God worship him, he also wasn't able to trick Jesus into worshiping him. But he has done an incredible job at tricking the creation of God into worshiping him through religion.

Satan is the author of the religious spirit and he uses this spirit to rule over man made churches in a form of godliness that denies the power. Religion has set itself up over many churches all over America and the world today. Churches controlled by the spirit of religion have no power, no authority, no signs, no wonders, no miracles, no answers and they're just a form of godliness with no power.

What are the signs of a narcissist?

- Exaggerated sense of self-importance - Many church leaders feel that they are the most knowledgeable person in the church and that they are to rule over every decision.

- Sense of entitlement and require constant, excessive admiration - Regardless of achievements many of the church leaders require you to identify them by specific titles, give them special parking, special seating and many other type privileges.

- Expect to be recognized as superior even without achievements that warrant it - Many church leaders desire to be exalted just simply upon their position.

- Exaggerate achievements and talents - Many church leaders will make you believe they have a much closer walk with God than the reality.

- Believe they are superior and can only associate with equally special people - Many times church leaders will associate with the ones that give the most to the church or have the most to offer.

- Control conversations and belittle or look down on people they perceive as inferior - Many church leaders like to impress with knowledge instead of leading and helping with wisdom.

- Take advantage of others to get what they want - Oftentimes church leaders use their position to get special favors such as free meals, car repair, yard work, home repairs and many other such things.

- Behave in an arrogant or haughty manner, coming across as conceited, boastful and pretentious - Many leaders dress the best and put themselves above the ones they are to serve.

- Insist on having the best of everything — for instance, the best car or office, houses way more expensive than needed, expensive clothing, extensive travel

Satan doesn't like to humble himself because he is full of pride. He always entices and offers things that are bigger than life. He's always getting others to chase the next big thing. Satan is never and will never be satisfied unless he is the focal point of worship and control.

Have you ever wondered why we don't see signs, wonders and miracles in the church today? Have you ever wondered why we don't experience the greater works Jesus said we would? I was praying and asking God why were we're not seeing these great and promised things and the Holy Spirit gave me revelation into what was wrong.

The Holy Spirit asked me, "if I recalled the scripture in Matthew 12:24-26 KJV "24 But when the Pharisees heard it, they said, This fellow doth not cast out devils, but by Beelzebub the prince of the devils. 25 And Jesus knew their thoughts, and said unto them, Every kingdom divided against itself is brought to desolation; and every city or house divided against itself shall not stand: 26 And if Satan cast out Satan, he is divided against himself; how shall then his kingdom stand?"

I said yes and the Holy Spirit began to explain and say, "You have learned that the spirit of religion controlling most churches in America is demonic in nature. If Satan is in the position of authority in church, why would he then cast himself out?" This was a massive moment of revelation to me, no wonder we are not seeing the true power of God and experiencing signs, wonders, and miracles in most churches today, God isn't even present. Many people are following the spirit of religion thinking they are actually following the Holy Spirit. Following a form of godliness that has no power.

Satan so desires to be worshiped he has falsely set himself up as an imposter in a building titled church and desires and demands to be worshiped. No wonder the Christian churches have over 45,000 different denominations as a house totally divided.

Satan has created a place of worship and his cycle of narcissistic abuse requires an audience of victims willing to fuel his ego. He roams like a lion seeking someone who will be the desire of his lies. He is always hunting for another victim. This is why so many people are hurt deeply by religion today. The author of religion is narcissistic and abuses his people followed by lies of love and compassion of bruises. The narcissist keeps his victim at the point of exhaustion and resuscitates them just in time for the next abuse just to feed his own selfish needs.

This is not how it was ever intended to be. God is not a religion. Jesus is not a religion or a religious leader. Jesus is a king and a king has a domain. When you read the New Testament it's all about the Kingdom of God. Jesus said in Matthew 6:33 "33 But seek ye first the kingdom of God, and his righteousness; and all these things shall be added unto you." If you're tired of the abuse, if you've given up, if you just know deep down inside there is something more than what you've seen in church "seek ye first the kingdom of God."

You were never meant to be a victim, to be abused, to be confused. Today is your day to break free from the lies of the narcissistic spirit of religion and its father Satan. I hope this has opened your eyes to the difference between religion and the kingdom of God. May God bless you and lead you in all of your ways. The narcissistic abuser has been exposed!

Made in the USA
Columbia, SC
04 February 2023

11044071R00022